BE THE RAINBOW

A PRACTICAL GUIDE FOR SUPPORTING BEREAVED CHILDREN IN PRIMARY SCHOOLS

Justin Bowen

Independently Published

Copyright © 2021 Justin Bowen

All rights reserved. No part of this publication may be reproduced, distributed, or transmitted in any form or by any means, including photocopying, recording, or other electronic or mechanical methods, without the prior written permission of the publisher, except in the case of brief quotations embodied in critical reviews and certain other non-commercial uses permitted by copyright law. For permission requests, email the publisher at info@betherainbow.co.uk
ISBN 978-1-9168746-2-6 (Paperback)

First printing edition 2022

With much appreciation for

Book Design:
Alison Keys Creative

Advice and Guidance:
Dr Louise Field, Kim S. Golding CBE,
Victoria Devonshire, Craig Westby and Claire Howitt.

INTRODUCTION

My children were 5 and 7 years old when their mum, my wife, died of cancer. It was a bewildering, turbulent time. But through the grief and the tears, we were blessed with wonderful support, in particular from the children's school. That support played a huge part in us coming through the weeks and months that followed in as good a shape as we could have hoped for.

A year or so later, my daughter painted a picture. There were clouds and rain, lots of rain, but also a rainbow. She said the clouds and the rain were like the storm she sometimes felt inside. I asked her what the rainbow was and she said it was all the things that made her feel better. Then I asked her what helped her feel better, and one of the things she said was school.

I had heard from other parents in my position that although many schools offered good support, there were also many that provided little to no support. Practice varied widely, so I decided to try and do something to help.

Working with my children's school and taking advice from other professionals and specialist bereavement services, I have put together this practical guide for Primary Schools, so that they too can BE THE RAINBOW

PURPOSE OF THIS GUIDE

"The death of a parent or sibling is one of the most fundamental losses a child will ever face." – A Child's Grief, Winston's Wish

For schools and teachers, it can be difficult to know how best to support a bereaved child and how to help them through one of the biggest challenges that child will face. The grieving process that a child goes through is complex and difficult. By providing the right support, a school can play an important part in helping that child learn to live with their loss, and in so doing become part of the healing process. By not doing so (as sadly sometimes happens), the school can make an already difficult process harder – and no school wishes to do that. So, the stakes are high.

Every child is different, and every bereavement is unique, so it is not practical to provide a "one size fits all" manual for schools to follow. Instead, this guide seeks to provide a toolkit of options from which Primary Schools can tailor individualised support plans for grieving children aged 6 to 10. This book includes templates and activities for schools to use where appropriate and also sets out some of the key principles that plans should be based on. In this guide I refer to these plans as Bereavement Support Plans, to distinguish them from other support plans that schools may have for non-grieving children. This highlights the unique challenges grieving children face.

THIS GUIDE AIMS TO HELP PRIMARY SCHOOLS:

- Understand how children grieve.
- Respond effectively when a child experiences the death of someone important.
- Assess a child's needs for returning to education following bereavement.
- Develop a Bereavement Support Plan
- Implement the plan
- Keep the plan under review
- Seek further support, resources and training where appropriate.

The aim, ultimately, is to help a primary school faced with the challenge of supporting a grieving child to "BE THE RAINBOW"

PURPOSE OF THIS GUIDE

ASSESS

RESPOND PLAN IMPLEMENT

UNDERSTAND REVIEW SEEK

CONTENTS

- **6** How children aged 6 to 10 grieve.
- **8** Responding to the child and family when death is imminent or has just happened.
- **11** Assessing the child's needs for resuming education.
- **14** The Bereavement Support Plan: key principles.
- **17** The Bereavement Support Plan: common themes.
- **30** Appendices.
- **31** References and further reading.

HOW CHILDREN AGED 6 TO 10 GRIEVE

The way children grieve can be different to an adult. It has been described that a child's grief is like jumping in puddles – they jump in and out, one minute feeling their loss acutely, the next playing happily or wanting to know what is for tea! Being aware of these sudden shifts in attention can help adults in how they respond to the child. When the child is in their grief, hold them emotionally, but be ready to allow them to be children too. There are specific behaviours associated with children's grief that staff working with bereaved children should consider.

EMOTIONAL TURBULENCE

At this age children will normally be becoming more independent, but the death of someone important can destabilise them and make them more dependent on their family. It can leave them feeling unsafe and not knowing their place in the world. This can impact their ability to manage their feelings, causing mood swings and big emotional releases. Anger and distress are common for children at this age, which might be scary for both the child themselves and those around them. Thoughts and feelings can fluctuate, and they might say things which are uncomfortable for others to hear. All of this is normal and can be helped by including relevant activities in the Behaviour Support Plan.

FEELING DIFFERENT

The death of a parent might make the child feel different to everybody else at a time when they are forming relationships with peers and wanting to fit in. The child might have difficulty expressing such feelings and as a result it can affect their interactions with other children – they might isolate themselves or become more aggressive. Letting the child know that you understand they are struggling is helpful at such times. Explain that their behaviour is a normal response to losing someone important, but equally that their behaviour matters.

The Behaviour Support Plan can include activities to help the child identify and express their feelings.

FANTASIES ABOUT DEATH

Within this age range, children have at least some awareness of the finality of death and how death can impact them. However, they may still fantasise about being able to go and see their loved one again and might talk about wanting to die so that they can be with them. They might see death as something frightening or imagine the person coming back as a ghost or zombie and may also have bad dreams.

All of this is normal and is part of the child coming to terms with their loss. It is important that such thoughts and feelings are acknowledged and that the child is reassured that this is normal and something that many children experience when they lose someone important. It can be helpful to gently explain that although nobody really knows what happens to someone when they die, we do know that they do not come back.

RESPONDING TO THE CHILD & FAMILY WHEN A DEATH IS IMMINENT OR HAS JUST HAPPENED

How a school responds in those initial hours and days can significantly affect the relationship the school has with the child and their family. What should a school do when they become aware that a death has happened or is about to happen? In most cases, a simple phone call home is a good way to begin.

What is said in that initial call will partly depend on the circumstances. Was death sudden or expected? Were there aspects that were particularly traumatic (e.g. suicide, victim of murder)? In all circumstances, schools should be mindful of the long-term relationship with the child and their family. Generally, the following will be helpful:

- Above all else, show that you care.

- Keep it simple, just be supportive.

- Provide reassurance: let the child and their family know that you will do what you can to help, that their needs and wishes are paramount and not to worry about school work (it can be caught up!).

- Let the child know they can return to school when they are ready and that they can change their mind. It can be helpful to ask if they have any initial thoughts or feelings about returning to school (this will give an early indication of when that might be – it could be immediately).

- Be available: let the child and family know that they can contact you at any time (identify specific members of staff who they can liaise with)

Over the days that follow, many children and families will appreciate a card, a letter, flowers, attendance at the funeral. Such gestures will show that you understand and care about their loss.

RESPONDING TO DEATH

- PROVIDE REASSURANCE
- KEEP IT SIMPLE
- SCHOOL WHEN READY
- BE AVAILABLE
- SHOW YOU CARE

ASSESSING THE CHILD'S NEEDS FOR RESUMING EDUCATION

Some children will want to return to school quickly (in some cases the next day), while others may not be ready to return for a significant amount of time or even at all, in which case home schooling may need to be considered. In any event, the school will need to liaise with the family to assess the child's educational needs as they grieve and to develop a Bereavement Support Plan.

As with so much of this process, there is no one-size-fits-all approach as much will depend on the child and their family. However, using the **Bereavement Support Assessment** template found in **Appendix A** can provide a useful framework from which to build an effective support plan.

Additionally, when completing an assessment, there is good practice that can help:

- Identify a specific person for leading the assessment and liaising with the child and family, as well as any relevant external services which are involved. Having a single point of contact ensures clear communication and prevents the family having to repeat information, which can be painful and traumatic.

- Where possible and appropriate, visit the child and family in their own home to carry out the initial assessment. Two members of staff attending is ideal – one to lead the assessment, the other to assist and support the child and family.

- Be clear what information is needed and why - the aim is to make sure the child and family get the best possible support.

- Where external services are involved, ensure that relevant information they have is included in the assessment, with permission sought from the parent/carer in advance. Explain which members of staff, either in school or in external services, will have sight of the assessment.

- Explain what the Bereavement Support Plan is and what it is for and give reassurance that the child's needs come first.

- Let the child and family know that the Bereavement Support Plan will be developed at their own pace – there is no rush. Equally highlight any areas that might need to be covered initially (such as whether to let other children and parents know what has happened).

At the end of the initial assessment, it is helpful to give the child and family a timescale within which a draft version of the Bereavement Support Plan will be ready for them to see. Then, once the draft Bereavement Support Plan is ready, show and explain it to the child and family and ensure any changes they wish to make are considered.

Once the final version is complete, provide the child and family with a copy to keep. If appropriate a copy should also be given to any external services involved. Explain how the Bereavement Support Plan will be kept under review and if applicable make an appointment for a review meeting.

ASSESSING THE CHILD'S NEEDS FOR RESUMING EDUCATION

- BE CLEAR
- HOME VISIT
- INCLUDE EXTERNAL SERVICES
- CHILD FIRST
- NO RUSH
- IDENTIFY LEAD PERSON

THE BEREAVEMENT SUPPORT PLAN: KEY PRINCIPLES

The aim of a Bereavement Support Plan is to help a child in their grieving process within the school environment or in their home learning. To be effective, there are a number of principles which apply:

- Following a death, events can happen very quickly. It is a huge change in a child and family's life and thoughts and feelings can fluctuate and change constantly in the early days and weeks. It is therefore not essential for a Bereavement Support Plan to immediately be completed in full. There will be aspects which require time to plan and refine. However, the school should begin the planning process at the earliest opportunity as the child may wish to return to school quickly. A **Bereavement Support Plan Template** can be found in **Appendix B**.

- For a Bereavement Support Plan to be effective, it requires buy-in from all involved. It should therefore be a collaboration between the school, the child, the child's family and any support services that are involved.

- The needs of the child comes first.

- When a child's emotional needs are met, they will be much better placed to engage in education. The Bereavement Support Plan should therefore prioritise emotional support over academic learning, while also providing an educational framework which helps the child continue learning to the best of their ability while grieving.

- The familiarity of school routines and structure can be a reassuring anchor to a bereaved child. However, the emotional turbulence that grief brings means that it is also important to build flexibility into a **Bereavement Support Plan** to allow for the inevitable fluctuations in the child's mood, concentration and motivation.

THE BEREAVEMENT SUPPORT PLAN: KEY PRINCIPLES

- BUY IN FROM ALL
- BUILD OVER TIME
- CHILD FIRST
- EMOTIONAL OVER ACADEMIC
- STRUCTURE WITH FLEXIBILITY

THE BEREAVEMENT SUPPORT PLAN: COMMON THEMES

Each bereaved child will have their own needs and wishes, so every Bereavement Support Plan will be unique. However, there are common themes which it is helpful to build a support plan around. These themes are listed below and are included in The Bereavement Support Plan template found in Appendix B.

Exactly what support will be included should be determined by the needs identified in The Bereavement Support Assessment.

- Returning to school
- Emotional
- Educational
- Behavioural
- Safeguarding
- Home learning
- Support during change

THE BEREAVEMENT SUPPORT PLAN: COMMON THEMES

- EDUCATIONAL
- EMOTIONAL
- BEHAVIOURAL
- SAFEGUARDING
- HOMELEARNING
- SUPPORTING CHANGE
- RETURNING TO SCHOOL

THE BEREAVEMENT SUPPORT PLAN: COMMON THEMES

RETURNING TO SCHOOL

TIMING

Does the child wish to return to school at this moment, and if so, does that mean full-time, part-time or with a phased return? Again, there is no definitive rule as to what is best – every circumstance is unique. However, it is helpful to be clear as to which hours the child will attend initially and how that can be adapted where appropriate.

Options to consider are:

- Immediate full-time attendance, but with the option to return home during the school day if necessary.
- Full-time attendance, but with flexibility around arrival time in the morning. Sometimes simply avoiding the school rush can be enough to help the child settle into the school routine.
- Full-time attendance but with specific emotional support at the start of the school day (such as going into a nurture group) or during other periods which the child might be worried about (such as lunchtime).
- Phased return, with the child starting on reduced hours and building up attendance over time.

As with all aspects of the Bereavement Support Plan, this should be kept under constant review and changed where necessary.

LETTING THE COMMUNITY KNOW WHAT HAS HAPPENED.

Following a death, the child may not want to constantly be explaining what has happened and potentially reliving their loss, nor will the parent on the "school run" want to be constantly answering questions. Additionally, children often tease each other about being different and a bereavement is no exception. As part of the community, the school can play a part in ensuring accurate information is disseminated, preventing rumours and inuendo. Equally, other parents can be very sympathetic and helpful and letting them know can result in the family receiving unexpected but valuable support. Classmates and school friends can play an important role in helping the child in their return to school, providing emotional support as well as much needed laughter and fun. Knowing that everyone has a clear understanding of what has happened and experiencing positive responses from peers can reduce the risk of a child feeling embarrassed or ashamed.

So, with this in mind and with the permission of the child and their family, the school is ideally placed to let the community know what has happened. How this is done will depend on many factors, but one or more of the following may be appropriate:

- Write to other parents letting them know what has happened. To ensure that no parent is missed out, consider more than one format (e.g. letter and email).

- Let the school know as part of an assembly. It is important after the announcement that some time is allowed before children return to normal lessons, so that questions can be answered, and any support given.

- In individual classes, ask the teacher to explain in a clear and factual way what has happened. Letting other children know how the child might be feeling and encouraging friends to be openly supportive can be immensely helpful.

Whichever method is used, it is important for staff to plan how the information is delivered and to allow for further information and support to be provided to those who may need it.

Use simple, factual, honest language that is age appropriate. It is ok to say a little about how the person died where appropriate, whether by an accident (e.g. a car accident), or through illness (e.g. cancer, heart-attack). Giving a little explanation to help children understand can also be helpful (e.g. "We need our hearts to work properly as they have the important job of sending blood around our body. Mr Smith died because he had an illness which meant his heart stopped working and although the doctors tried to make it better, they could not.").

It is also good to acknowledge the feelings that children may experience on hearing what has happened. E.g. "Some of you might feel sad or worried about this news, or you might not feel anything at all. Its ok to have these feelings and its normal. If you want to talk about what has happened, or want to cry, or if you want to share happy memories about Mr Smith then that is ok too, and we are here for you. If you have any questions, we will do our best to answer those too."

ENSURING ALL RELEVANT STAFF ARE AWARE OF THE BEREAVMENT SUPPORT PLAN.

It is important that as part of the transition back into school, all relevant staff are made aware of the arrangements in place for the child's return. This is particularly important around hours of attendance and variations in the child's timetable. Similarly, making sure that letters home are addressed appropriately is also important - a bereaved parent may be sensitive to receiving letters from school addressed to both parents.

THE BEREAVEMENT SUPPORT PLAN: COMMON THEMES
EMOTIONAL SUPPORT

This is perhaps the most important part of The Bereavement Support Plan. Children spend most of their waking day at school and part of that day will inevitably be spent remembering and thinking about the person who has died and experiencing the range of emotions that grief brings. The emotional support that a school can provide to help a child is wide ranging. There are however a few key principles to this:

- Make the school environment a safe and supportive place to be.

- Help the child manage their fluctuating emotions and moods

- Show that the school understands and cares about the child's loss

The following are ways in which the child can be emotionally supported in school:

THE CHILD'S CLASSROOM
Treasuring memories is an important part of a child's grief, and it is helpful for a grieving child to have reminders of that person easily accessible to them. Displaying a photo of the person who has died in a classroom where a child spends much of their time is a good way of doing this. Having a nice frame, perhaps which the child has decorated and added a message to adds to this.

HELPING THE CHILD IDENTIFY AND EXPRESS FEELINGS
The emotions that grief brings can be turbulent and frightening for

anyone, especially children. Children will often need help to recognise and to let others know when they are having a hard time. Letting children know that it is normal to have lots of different feelings when someone has died and that it is good to ask for help is an important part of this. Some examples of activities to do this are as follows (see Appendix C):

- Jar of Memories
- Feelings Volcano
- There for Me
- Feelings First Aid Kit

EMOTIONAL SUPPORT PROPS

It is often helpful for a child to have items available from which they can take comfort through the day. This might be something from home that they take comfort from, such as a special teddy. However, to prevent a comforter becoming a distraction, it may be helpful to include a few simple rules around its use in the Bereavement Support Plan. For example, having a place in the classroom where the comforter will "live" when it's not needed or when it's time to learn.

Equally, a child might take comfort from items which help them remember the person who has died. Having mementoes kept together in a memory box or bag that the child can access whenever they need to can be helpful. An exercise to create a Memory Box can be found in Appendix D.

NURTURE TIME

Allowing the child to have dedicated time out for emotional support when they need to can be helpful. This can be both in a structured way, with a regular time allocated as part of the child's timetable, and as required when the child feels they are struggling. A card which they can show when they are finding it difficult to manage should be part of that. During these periods, it is helpful if there is someone available for the child to talk to or to engage the child in emotionally supportive activities, so it is good to specify who and where in the Bereavement Support Plan.

MARKING SPECIAL DAYS

Special days, such as birthdays and anniversaries, can be especially hard for children when someone important in a family has died. It does help to plan and prepare openly for days which are known to be challenging. As part of the assessment for developing the Bereavement Support Plan, it can be helpful to identify all the important dates throughout the year when the child might be thinking about the person who has died. Include personal dates (such as birthdays and anniversaries) as well as national days, such as Mothers' Day or Fathers' Day.

As the day approaches, plan with the child if and how they would like to mark it. Even if the child does not wish to specifically recognise the day, it may still be important for a teacher to "check in" with the child when the time comes.

FACILITATING THERAPEUTIC INPUT

Most children and families will be able to cope when someone important dies. However, there may come a time, often long after a person has died, when a child would benefit from more specialist bereavement support. This may be initiated by the child's family, support services or the school itself.

Whichever way this therapeutic input is instigated, many bereavement support services wish to see the child at the school. It is important that in such circumstances the school works in partnership with the service provider to facilitate this, usually by making a room available and having any appointments built into the child's timetable. Including this partnership work in the Bereavement Support Plan makes the school's role clear.

EMOTIONAL SUPPORT

- CLASSROOM
- HELP WITH FEELINGS
- EMOTIONAL PROPS
- NURTURE TIME
- SPECIAL DAYS
- FACILITATE THERAPY

THE BEREAVEMENT SUPPORT PLAN: COMMON THEMES
EDUCATIONAL

Children are resilient and although a grieving child will experience a range of emotions, it is important not to underestimate their ability to continue learning.

Inevitably there will be times when academic learning has to take a back seat, when a child's concentration and motivation are impacted by emotional turbulence – indeed teachers should expect educational progress to stall or even go backwards for a period after a child loses someone important.

It is normal for working memory to be impaired after trauma, although it does recover in time, but this may mean spelling tests etc. prove particularly challenging. However, learning will resume as healing begins and by putting in place some simple measures the school can help a child through difficult moments.

Including these measures in the **Bereavement Support Plan** will help the child focus on continuing their education with their peers, which in turn will help their self-esteem.

Some examples of educational support tools are as follows
(see Appendix E)

- My Daily Timetable
- Now and Next Board

It may also be necessary to help a bereaved child catch up on work they have missed, although there is a balance to be found so that no undue pressure is placed on the child. It can be useful for the school to include any additional educational support that will be provided in the **Bereavement Support Plan**.

Another area for schools to be mindful of is around homework. Again, there is a balance to be found between allowing the child to continue to function normally and not placing undue pressure on them or their family. Schools will have their own approach to homework and generally, homework should continue to be set as normal, but with an understanding that it may not always be completed, or perhaps making time available to finish it at school. Whatever is agreed, a simple statement in the Bereavement Support Plan about homework can help ease the pressure.

BEHAVIOURAL

The familiarity of school, its routines and its structure can reassure a grieving child that some things have not changed, so maintaining rules and boundaries is important. However, it is also true that with the emotional turbulence that grief brings there may well be changes in a child's behaviour. They may seek to test rules, boundaries, and teachers to reassure themselves that they can still be relied upon.

Sometimes the emotions grieving children experience may be so big that they have outbursts of anger or sadness. All feelings are acceptable, and appropriate, and should be acknowledged, although children need help dealing with the behaviours that they cause. Reasonable allowances should be made where appropriate, while also letting the child know that rules still apply. Helping the child to recognise and show when they are finding it difficult to should be part of that.

THE BEREAVEMENT SUPPORT PLAN: COMMON THEMES

SAFEGUARDING

Where a child who is vulnerable, or who has safeguarding services already involved, loses someone important, then how safeguarding concerns will be communicated should also be included in the Bereavement Support Plan.

HOME LEARNING

Sometimes it may take time before a child is ready to return to school, or it might be that a child finds being in school too much for a particular period of time. In such cases, the school should consider supporting the child continuing education at home until such time as they are ready to return. Maintaining regular contact with the child and their family during this period is important so that the school can be ready to welcome the child back when they are ready.

SUPPORT DURING CHANGE

Having experienced such a big change in their life, some children who have lost someone important may find further moments of change particularly challenging. It is good to pay particular attention to the child's needs during such periods, such as leaving school, moving to a new home, the end of therapeutic input, important friends or teachers leaving. During times of significant change, it may be helpful to sit with the child and review the Bereavement Support Plan to see if any additional support is needed.

REVIEWING THE BEREAVEMENT SUPPORT PLAN

It is important to keep the Bereavement Support Plan under review to ensure that it remains relevant and so that it can be adapted as the child's feelings and needs change. It is also important to ensure on-going, open communication between all involved to allow for concerns to be raised, positives to be built-on and changes to be made efficiently. To support this, the Bereavement Support Plan should identify lead professionals and the best way to contact them. It may also be useful to set out arrangements for formally reviewing the Bereavement Support Plan, such as by holding a quarterly review.

APPENDICES

Appendix A – Bereavement Support Assessment Template
Appendix B – Bereavement Support Plan Template
Appendix C – Activities for Helping A Child Identify
 and Express their Feelings

- Jar of Memories
- Feelings Volcano
- There for Me! Bracelet
- Feelings First Aid Kit

Appendix D – Emotional Support Props:
- Making a Memory Box

Appendix E – Educational Support Tools
- My Daily Timetable
- Now and Next Board

APPENDIX A

BEREAVEMENT SUPPORT ASSESSMENT TEMPLATE

BE THE RAINBOW
BEREAVEMENT SUPPORT ASSESSMENT

BEREAVEMENT SUPPORT ASSESSMENT TEMPLATE; GUIDANCE NOTES

The aim of the Bereavement Support Assessment is to identify the child's needs for returning to education and to inform the Bereavement Support Plan. Please also see the section "Assessing the child's needs for resuming education" in Be The Rainbow for good practice when carrying out the assessment.

GENERAL INFORMATION
This is the core personal information needed about the child and their parent/carer.

HEALTH AND WELL-BEING
This section assesses the child's physical and mental health, where the child is struggling with emotions related to their bereavement, activities set out in Appendix C can be included in The Bereavement Support Plan to help. However, where significant mental health issues are identified then the school should make referrals to specialist agencies, in line with good practice.

BEREAVEMENT DETAILS & PROTECTIVE FACTORS
The cause and circumstances of death will affect the child's immediate response to their important person dying. For example, my wife's death came after several years of living with cancer, so the children had some preparation for when the time came, including having been encouraged to express their feelings. This meant that although their grief was still profound, it wasn't compounded with the shock and trauma that a sudden death can bring. However, for some children the death may bring trauma which will need particular attention.

Additionally, a child's understanding of what death means is relevant in that it will give an indication as to how able they are to process what has happened and their ability to identify and express their feelings. This may well be linked to the circumstances around the death.

It is also important to identify protective factors which can form the foundation of their bereavement support. For example existing friendships, activities and clubs they already enjoy and good relationships with teachers can all be important in helping grieving children - indeed their close friends may well prove to be their biggest source of support. The Bereavement Support Plan should be build on these by including exercises such as 'There for Me!' 'Bracelet' and 'Feeling First Aid Kit'.

IMPORTANT DATES
These are dates which may have particular significance for the child in respect of the person who died. The child may not wish to "do" anything specific on these dates, but it is important for the school to be aware of them, even if it is just to make a point of checking with the child how they are on those days. The child's wishes around these dates should be included in the Bereavement Support Plan.

BEREAVEMENT ASSESSMENT
GENERAL INFORMATION

CHILD'S NAME:

DATE OF BIRTH:

CLASS TEACHER:

SCHOOL YEAR:

PARENT / CARER NAME:

RELATIONSHIP:

ADDRESS:

POSTCODE:

EMAIL:

PHONE:

ETHNICITY:

GENDER:

PRIMARY LANGUAGE:

RELIGION:

SIBLINGS & AGES (IF APPLICABLE):

HEALTH & WELL-BEING

G.P. NAME & ADDRESS:

DOES THE CHILD HAVE SEN, A REGISTERED DISABILITY, LONG-TERM ILLNESS, OR ANY OTHER DIAGNOSED CONDITION?

DOES THE CHILD HAVE ANY ALLERGIES?

IS THE CHILD ON ANY MEDICATION?

HOW IS THE CHILD SLEEPING?

HOW IS THE CHILD EATING?

HOW IS THE CHILDS MENTAL HEALTH?

ARE THERE ANY OTHER HEALTH CONCERNS?

IS THE CHILD RECEIVING SUPPORT FROM SOCIAL SERVICES OR ANY OTHER AGENCIES

BEREAVEMENT DETAILS & PROTECTIVE FACTORS

NAME OF PERSON WHO DIED:

RELATIONSHIP TO CHILD:

DATE OF DEATH:

CAUSE & CIRCUMSTANCES OF DEATH:

WHEN & WHERE WILL / DID FUNERAL TAKE PLACE?

DOES THE CHILD HAVE ANY INITIAL THOUGHTS ABOUT RETURNING TO SCHOOL?

WOULD THE CHILD & FAMILY LIKE THE SCHOOL TO LET THE SCHOOL COMMUNITY (INCLUDING PUPILS, PARENTS AND STAFF) KNOW ABOUT THE PERSON DYING?

IF YES, IS THERE ANY INFORMATION THEY DO NOT WISH TO BE SHARED?

WHO ARE THE CHILD'S BEST FRIENDS AT SCHOOL?

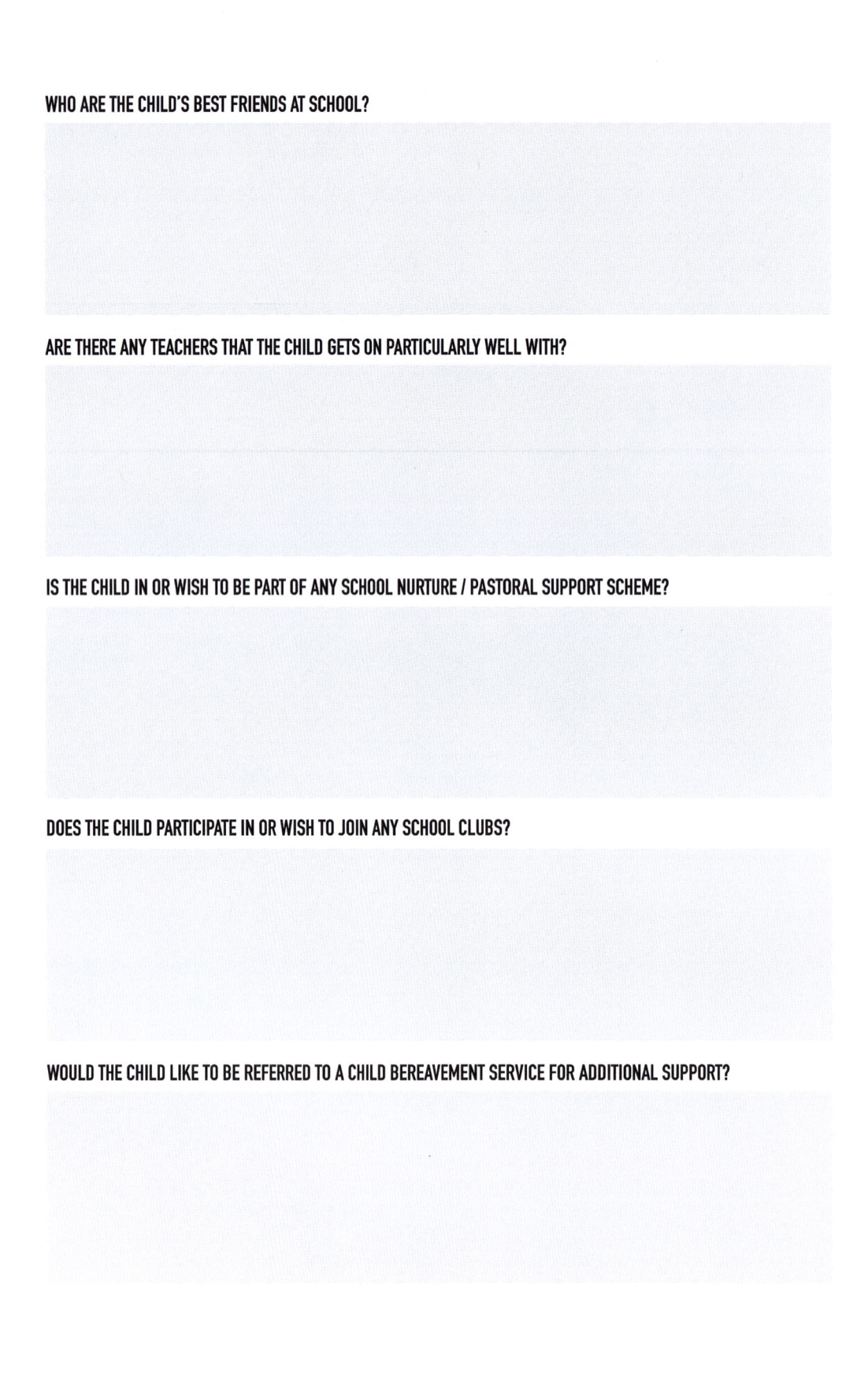

ARE THERE ANY TEACHERS THAT THE CHILD GETS ON PARTICULARLY WELL WITH?

IS THE CHILD IN OR WISH TO BE PART OF ANY SCHOOL NURTURE / PASTORAL SUPPORT SCHEME?

DOES THE CHILD PARTICIPATE IN OR WISH TO JOIN ANY SCHOOL CLUBS?

WOULD THE CHILD LIKE TO BE REFERRED TO A CHILD BEREAVEMENT SERVICE FOR ADDITIONAL SUPPORT?

IMPORTANT DATES

ARE THERE ANY OF THE FOLLOWING DATES WHICH THE CHILD OR FAMILY FEEL MIGHT BE DIFFICULT OR THAT THEY WANT THE SCHOOL TO BE AWARE OF JUST IN CASE?

ANNIVERSARY OF DEATH

DECEASED PERSON'S BIRTHDAY

CHILD'S BIRTHDAY

MOTHER'S / FATHER'S DAY

CHRISTMAS

ANY OTHER IMPORTANT DATES:

IS THERE ANYTHING ELSE THE CHILD OR FAMILY WOULD LIKE THE SCHOOL TO KNOW, INCLUDING ANY CULTURAL OR RELIGIOUS MATTERS THE SCHOOL SHOULD BE AWARE OF?

IS THERE ANYTHING ELSE THE CHILD OR FAMILY WOULD LIKE THE SCHOOL TO DO IF POSSIBLE?

APPENDIX B

BEREAVEMENT SUPPORT PLAN TEMPLATE

BE THE RAINBOW
BEREAVEMENT SUPPORT PLAN

BEREAVEMENT SUPPORT PLAN

GENERAL INFORMATION

CHILD'S NAME:

DATE OF BIRTH:

NAME OF PARENT/CARER:

RELATIONSHIP:

HOME ADDRESS:

POSTCODE:

EMAIL ADDRESS:

PHONE:

CLASS TEACHER:

SCHOOL YEAR:

TEACHER(S) RESPONSIBLE FOR PLAN:

EMAIL ADDRESS:

PHONE:

RETURNING TO SCHOOL
(E.G. WHEN, HOURS, LETTING THE COMMUNITY KNOW)

EMOTIONAL – HELP WITH FEELINGS
(E.G. CLASSROOM, ACTIVITIES, SUPPORT PROPS, SPECIAL DATES, THERAPY)

EDUCATIONAL – HELP WITH LEARNING
(E.G. MY DAILY TIMETABLE, NOW AND NEXT, EXTRA HELP, HOMEWORK)

BEHAVIOURAL – HELP BEHAVIOUR
(E.G. NURTURE TIME)

SAFEGUARDING
WHAT WE'LL DO IF WE'RE WORRIED ABOUT YOU

HOME LEARNING
WHAT WE'LL DO IF YOU NEED TO LEARN FROM HOME

HELP IF THINGS CHANGE
(E.G. MOVING SCHOOL OR HOUSE)

REVIEW – CHECKING THE PLAN IS HELPING
(E.G. WHO TO CONTACT IF SOMETHING ISN'T WORKING, NEXT REVIEW MEETING)

ANYTHING ELSE WE NEED TO DO

ARE WE ALL HAPPY WITH WHAT'S IN THE PLAN?

CHILD'S NAME:

SIGNED: **DATE:**

PARENT/CARER'S NAME:

RELATIONSHIP TO CHILD:

SIGNED: **DATE:**

TEACHERS NAME:

SIGNED: **DATE:**

APPENDIX C

ACTIVITIES FOR HELPING A CHILD IDENTIFY AND EXPRESS THEIR FEELINGS

JAR OF MEMORIES

WHAT IS THIS ACTIVITY FOR?

Acknowledging that someone has died and then acknowledging the thoughts and feelings that go with that is an important step in the grieving process. The Jar of Memories can represent some of the thoughts and feelings the child has and help them in expressing these.

WHAT YOU WILL NEED

A Small Clean Jar with a Screw Top Lid,
Packet of Table Salt,
Coloured Chalk or Pastels,
Cotton Wool Ball,
5 pieces of A4 paper.

HOW TO DO IT

Begin by explaining that each different colour in the jar well represent a thought or feeling that the child has had since the person died. Explain that, whether happy or sad, their feelings are important.

Ask the child to think about a feeling they have. Then ask them to think of a thought that goes with that feeling, for example "Sadness, I feel sad at night when Mummy isn't there to cuddle me.", or "Scared, I'm scared in case something happens to Dad and I'm left alone.", or "Happy, I'm happy that I still have my Dad and brother.". Write it down on one of the pieces of A4 paper. Reassure the child that all feelings are appropriate when a person they care about has died.

Repeat until the child has done this for 5 feelings - there should be a different feeling written on each piece of paper. Then, help the child decide on a colour for each feeling and mark that colour next to the writing on the relevant piece of paper.
Fill the jar right up to the brim with salt, making sure it is jammed full. This gives the exact amount of salt needed. Then help the child to tip the salt out of the jar into 5 piles on the 5 pieces of paper. Each of these piles will represent a feeling, so explain to the child they can make piles of equal sizes or, if some feelings are more significant to them, have some bigger than others.

Then ask the child to take the matching coloured chalk or pastel for a feeling and rub it into the relevant pile of salt. As they rub it in, the salt will begin to turn to that colour. They'll need to keep rubbing in a circular motion until it is the colour they want. Repeat until each pile is coloured.

Then help the child to carefully tip the salt, one pile at a time, into the jar. This can be done in straight layers or diagonals, however the child wishes it to look.

Once finished, tap the jar gently to settle the contents. Then put the cotton wool ball on top and screw the lid on tightly. The cotton wool stops the colours from mixing and forms a seal.

The jar is now ready for the child to share with anyone they wish, and to keep somewhere to remind them of all their different feelings.

JAR OF MEMORIES
CHILD'S EXPLANATION SHEET

When someone has died we can have lots of different thoughts and feelings. Whether they are happy or sad thoughts, all your feelings are important. The Jar of Memories can help us say what those thoughts and feelings are.

Each colour represents a thought or feeling, so it is up to you to decide if they are all equal, or if some will be bigger than others.

When you've finished your Jar of Memories, you might like to tell someone you trust what each colour represents.

Decide where you want to keep your jar, to remind you of all your different thoughts and feelings and to remember that it's OK to have them.

FEELINGS VOLCANO

WHAT IS THIS ACTIVITY FOR?
The Feelings Volcano is a metaphorical representation of a child's emotions. It helps show how there can be big emotions (the lava), which can come out in big ways (erupting).

WHAT YOU WILL NEED
Old Newspaper
2 Large pieces of Card
Coloured Paper
Paint
Glue
Sticky Tape

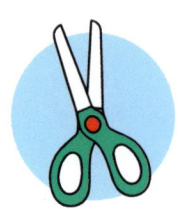

HOW TO DO IT
Scrunch the newspaper up into lots of balls about the size of a fist. Use one piece of card as the base, and start to glue the scrunched up

newspaper balls onto it, building them up into the shape of a volcano. Use lots of glue and sticky tape. When the volcano shape is made and the glue has dried, paint the volcano.

Next it's time to make the exploding lava. Make a template in the shape of a spiral on another piece of card then trace spirals onto different coloured paper. On each spiral complete any or all of the sentences on the child's explanation sheet, then cut them out and stick them onto the volcano (they can also add their own).

FEELINGS VOLCANO
CHILD'S EXPLANATION SHEET

Feelings can be explosive! When someone dies, you may have lots of different feelings and those feelings are bursting to get out. Talking to others sometimes helps, especially if someone has died in their family too. On the Feelings Volcano, the lava is the big emotions exploding to get out.

Fill out any of the feelings below, or even add your own, and write them on your lava:

I AM SCARED THAT...

I AM ANGRY ABOUT...

I GET CONFUSED WHEN...

I FEEL LONELY WHEN...

I AM WORRIED BECAUSE...

I FEEL SAD BECAUSE...

I FEEL EXCITED ABOUT...

I FEEL GUILTY BECAUSE...

I FEEL RELIEVED BECAUSE...

THERE FOR ME! BRACELET

WHAT IS THIS ACTIVITY FOR?
Bereaved children can feel lonely and that there isn't anyone they can talk to. The "There for Me" bracelet helps remind them about some of the people who care about them and who they can talk to about their feelings.

WHAT YOU WILL NEED:
At least 5 different Coloured Threads of the same length (Wool or Yarn are ideal),
Piece of Paper,
Pen or Pencil.

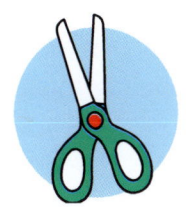

HOW TO DO IT:
To begin, ask the child to think of people who care about them and who they think they could talk to about their feelings. Some examples might be family, friends, a teacher or someone at a club they belong to. Write them down on the paper.

For each person on the list, ask the child to choose a different colour piece of thread. Tie all the threads together at one end and tape the knotted end to a table.

Help the child to twist or plait the threads together to make a pattern, then tie a knot in the open end. The bracelet is ready to wear.

THERE FOR ME! BRACELET
CHILD'S EXPLANATION SHEET

When somebody dies, you can feel very lonely. You might feel like there is no one who cares, or that there is no one to talk to. There are people in your family, friends, at school or clubs who do care and who would listen to you. It can be a good idea to remind yourself who these people are my making a friendship bracelet about all the people who are "There for Me!"

You can make lots of different bracelets in lots of different colours and patterns!

Just remember, it is ok to miss the person who died, but other people care about you too.

FEELINGS FIRST AID KIT

WHAT IS THIS ACTIVITY FOR?
The aim of the Feelings First Aid Kit is to help a child identify things that can help them feel better when they are struggling with difficult emotions or just having a bad day.

WHAT YOU WILL NEED
Shoe Box
Plain White Paper,
Paper for Drawing or Writing on
Colouring Pens
Glue.

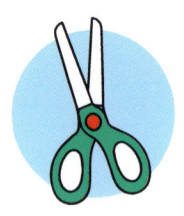

HOW TO DO IT
First, help the child to make the First Aid Box that they will keep the kit in. Cover the shoe box in white paper and on each side draw and colour

a simple, red cross. On the lid, the child can write "My Feelings First Aid Kit". Then make a list of the kind of things that would be found in a real first aid kit. This helps the child to think about things which can help when someone is hurt, or feeling bad, on the outside. Now take another piece of paper and ask the child to think about things that might help someone who is hurt on the inside, someone who is having a bad day. Make a list. Finally, help them to be creative and make, draw, or write about those things and to put them into their Feelings First Aid box.

FEELINGS FIRST AID KIT
CHILD'S EXPLANATION SHEET

When someone gets hurt on the outside, they might use a first aid kit to make themselves feel better. We can do the same if we are hurting on the inside - we can do things to make ourselves feel better when we're having a bad day.

What kind of things would you find in a real first aid kit? Make a list.

Now make a list of the things that might help if you are having a bad day.

Let's make, draw or write about them and put them in your very own feelings first aid kit!

APPENDIX D

EMOTIONAL SUPPORT PROPS: MAKING A MEMORY BOX

MAKING A MEMORY BOX

WHAT IS THIS ACTIVITY FOR?

Holding on to positive memories can be immensely helpful to bereaved children. Sometimes it can be helpful to keep special things connected with the person in a safe place, like a box, which children can add to whenever they want and also show other people if they wish. Memory Boxes can be bought which allow children to do this, or the child can make one. This exercise is one way of doing that.

WHAT YOU WILL NEED

A Box with a Lid,
Items to Decorate the Box with;
Paint, Crayons, Paper - be creative!

HOW TO DO IT

Explain to the child that a memory box is a safe place to keep and treasure all kinds of things that remind them of the person who died, and that they can decorate the box to make it personal to them. Help the child decorate the box, then let them know it is time to fill it. Explain they can put anything in it that will fit, but that they should check with other people in their family if they have photos or things that belonged to the person.

SOME IDEAS OF THINGS THEY MIGHT LIKE TO PUT IN ARE:
Photos, perfume or aftershave, cards, letters, small items of clothing (this can be sprayed with the person's perfume or aftershave), jewellery, CD of music, shells / cones / feathers found on a special walk. The child can also add labels to the items to tell their significance.

MAKING A MEMORY BOX
CHILD'S EXPLANATION SHEET

In a memory box you can keep all kinds of special things that remind you of the person who died and the times you spent together. You can decorate the box in all sorts of ways - be creative!

Anything that fits can go in the box - Photos, perfume or aftershave, cards, letters, small items of clothing (this can be sprayed with the person's perfume or aftershave), jewellery, CD of music, shells/cones/feathers found on a special walk.

Just remember to ask someone in your family if it's OK with them to put in photos or items that belonged to the person.

APPENDIX E

EDUCATIONAL SUPPORT TOOLS: MY DAILY TIMETABLE NOW AND NEXT BOARD

MY DAILY TIMETABLE

WHAT IS THIS ACTIVITY FOR?
All children benefit from the structure of a school day, and bereaved children are no exception. Having the day ahead set out simply and clearly provides the child with a welcome certainty amidst the turbulence of their grief.

WHAT YOU WILL NEED
A daily timetable chart
Pencils
Crayons.

HOW TO DO IT
Spend a few minutes with the child at the start of the day completing their daily timetable with them. This is also an opportunity to check out how they are feeling today and identify any issues that may have arisen.

MY DAILY TIMETABLE

TODAY IS	MORNING	PLAYTIME	LUNCHTIME	AFTERNOON	PLAYTIME	HOMETIME

NOW AND NEXT BOARD

WHAT IS THIS ACTIVITY FOR?
The aim of a Now and Next board is to help the child focus on what they are doing now, with the promise of a reward when the task is completed. As an example, my daughter wanted lots of cuddles in school, but this was often in the middle of an activity. By using the Now and Next board, it helped her concentrate on finishing her work first, with a cuddle when this was done.

WHAT YOU WILL NEED:
The Now and Next sheet attached and a pen.

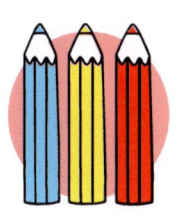

HOW TO DO IT:
Simply draw or write the activity that needs to be completed in the "Now" box, then draw or write the "reward" that the child will receive when the work is done in the "Next" box. It is important that the reward takes place as promised when the child has completed their task.

NOW AND NEXT

NOW

NEXT

REFERENCES AND FURTHER READING

The following material has been used in developing this guide:

A Child's Grief - Winston's Wish
A Guide to Supporting Young People in Education - Winston's Wish
Muddles, puddles and Sunshine - Winston's Wish
A Child's Questions about Death - Dignity Funeral Services

Further Reading:

"Working with relational trauma in schools: An educators guide to using dyadic development practice." - K.S. Golding, S. Philips, & L.M. Bomber
"Understanding Working Memory: A Classroom Guide" - Professor Susan E. Gathercole & Dr Tracey Packiam Alloway.

'Is It Still Ok To Have Cuddles?" - Elke Thompson
www.elkethompson.com

Additional Resources, Advice and Training:
www.winstonswish.org
www.childbereavementuk.org
www.nurturingmindsconsultancy.co.uk
www.kimsgolding.co.uk

For electronic copies of appendices, or for information on training, please email:

info@betherainbow.co.uk or visit: www.betherainbow.co.uk